Life's BIG Little Moments

GRANDFATHERS & GRANDCHILDREN

Life's BIG Little Moments

GRANDFATHERS & GRANDCHILDREN

SUSAN K. HOM

PHOTOGRAPHY BY JEFFREY H. MANTLER

STERLING

New York / London
www.sterlingpublishing.com

For my grandfathers, with love

STERLING and the distinctive Sterling logo are registered trademarks of
Sterling Publishing Co., Inc.

Library of Congress Cataloging-in-Publication Data

Hom, Susan K.   Life's big little moments: grandfathers & grandchildren / Susan K. Hom; photography by Jeffrey H. Mantler.
      p. cm.
    ISBN 978-1-4027-5839-3
1. Grandparent and child—Pictorial works. 2. Grandparent and child—Quotations, maxims, etc.   I. Title.
    HQ759.9.H659 2008 306.874'5--dc22

2008013405

10 9 8 7 6 5 4 3 2 1

Published by Sterling Publishing Co., Inc.
387 Park Avenue South, New York, NY 10016
© 2008 by Sterling Publishing Co., Inc.
Distributed in Canada by Sterling Publishing
C/o Canadian Manda Group, 165 Dufferin Street
Toronto, Ontario, Canada M6K 3H6
Distributed in the United Kingdom by GMC Distribution Services
Castle Place, 166 High Street, Lewes, East Sussex, England BN7 1XU
Distributed in Australia by Capricorn Link (Australia) Pty. Ltd.
P.O. Box 704, Windsor, NSW 2756, Australia

Printed in China
All rights reserved

Sterling ISBN 978-1-4027-5839-3

Page 11 photo: Peter Nurnberg
Pages 30–31 and 32 photos: Allison Horn
Page 36 photo: Linda Rotondo
Page 42 photo: Dean Johnson
Page 50 photo: © Michael Jang/Gettyimages.com

Page 61 photo: Christine Bulger
Page 73 photo: Julie Harrington
Pages 79 and 94 photos: Judee Herr
Page 82 photo: © Amy Eckert/Gettyimages.com

For information about custom editions, special sales, premium
and corporate purchases, please contact Sterling Special Sales
Department at 800-805-5489 or specialsales@sterlingpublishing.com.

Introduction

Whether it's on an early-morning fishing trip or an
adventurous piggyback ride, grandfathers know how to have fun.
Grandfathers get excited when the ice cream truck comes around,
and they know the importance of sound effects when it
comes to bedtime stories. At the same time, grandfathers can
always be relied upon as a source of comfort, support,
wisdom, and inspiration.

Grandchildren are easy to adore, from their spontaneous hugs
to their delightful giggles. Full of wonder, they can make a game out
of anything and are extremely curious about the world around them.
With their energy and enthusiasm, grandchildren encourage
grandfathers to be young at heart and are an
endless source of amusement.

The bond between grandfathers and grandchildren
is like no other and grows stronger through the years.
In all of life's BIG little moments, grandfathers and grandchildren
relish their time together and simply adore
one another unconditionally.

Grandchildren

show off their swimming skills to grandfathers.

Grandfathers

are always right there to cheer grandchildren on.

Grandchildren

bring grandfathers great happiness.

Grandfathers

encourage grandchildren to be confident.

Grandfathers introduce granddaughters

to the joys of reading.

Granddaughters help grandfathers

turn the page.

Grandchildren

help grandfathers make dinner.

Grandfathers

teach grandchildren the dos and don'ts

of table manners.

Grandfathers entertain grandchildren

with exciting stories at bedtime.

Grandchildren help grandfathers

make the animal noises.

Grandchildren remind grandfathers

to be adventurous.

Grandfathers help grandchildren

begin with small steps.

Grandfathers

hug grandchildren when they are feeling shy.

Grandchildren

find reassurance in the arms of grandfathers.

Grandfathers show grandchildren

where they work.

Grandchildren ask grandfathers

if they are superheroes.

Grandchildren inspire grandfathers

to be youthful.

Grandfathers help grandchildren

see the world from a new perspective.

—

Grandchildren remind grandfathers

how fun it is to try new things.

Grandfathers teach grandchildren

how to steer clear of the trees.

Grandchildren challenge grandfathers

to a game of one-on-one.

Grandfathers tell grandchildren

to not let anyone stand in the way

of their success.

Grandfathers

spend rainy days laughing with grandchildren.

Grandchildren

stomp in the puddles with grandfathers.

Grandfathers join grandchildren

in an afternoon snooze.

Grandchildren remind grandfathers

how refreshing a nap can be.

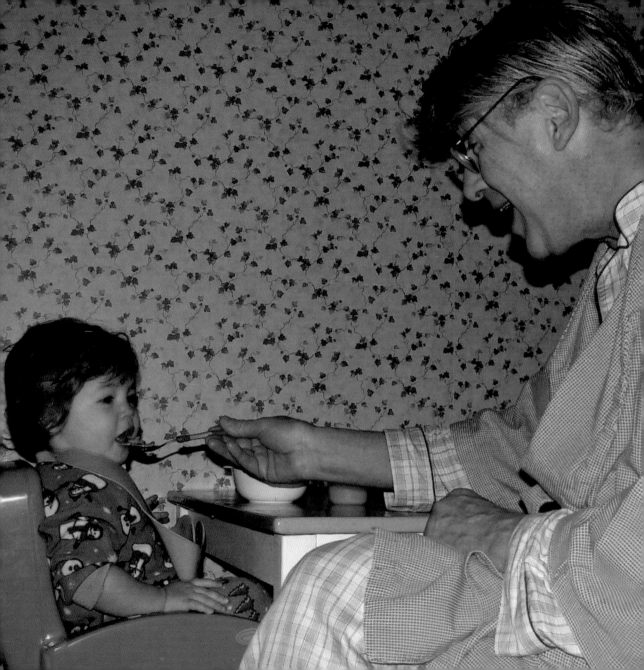

Grandfathers coax grandchildren

into eating all of their breakfast.

Grandchildren beg grandfathers

to pretend the spoon is an airplane.

Grandfathers

teach grandsons how to be gentlemen.

Grandsons

look to grandfathers for inspiration.

Grandfathers teach grandchildren

how to reel in a catch.

Grandchildren sometimes ask grandfathers

for help with the big ones.

Grandfathers remind grandchildren

that grown-ups play with toys, too.

Grandchildren beg grandfathers

to take them for a ride one day.

Grandchildren show grandfathers

their amazing soccer moves.

Grandfathers teach grandchildren

to always be gracious—in victory *and* defeat.

Grandchildren thank grandfathers

for their support.

Grandfathers remind grandchildren

to rejoice in every day.

Grandfathers show grandchildren

how much fun it is to splash around in the waves.

Grandchildren inspire grandfathers

to delight in feeling old pleasures renewed.

Grandchildren keep grandfathers

hip to new trends.

Grandfathers teach grandchildren

that some things never go out of style.

Grandchildren make grandfathers

beam with pride.

Grandfathers remind grandchildren

to savor precious moments.

Grandfathers inspire grandchildren

to be curious about everything.

Grandchildren remind grandfathers

that there is wisdom in youth.

Grandfathers

guide grandchildren through all of
life's ups and downs.

Grandchildren

have complete faith in grandfathers.

Grandfathers ask grandchildren

to help around the house.

Grandchildren think

there's nothing their grandfathers can't do.

Grandfathers remind grandchildren

that it's important to be patient.

Grandchildren ask grandfathers

to tell them about the biggest fish they ever caught.

Grandsons ask grandfathers

for pointers.

Grandfathers tell grandsons

to give it all they've got.

Grandfathers introduce grandchildren

to the joys of swinging.

Grandchildren give grandfathers

a helpful push.

Grandchildren ask grandfathers

lots of questions.

Grandfathers encourage grandchildren

to appreciate and respect the environment.

Grandfathers

tell grandchildren about when they

used to play football.

Grandchildren

hope to follow in grandfathers' footsteps.

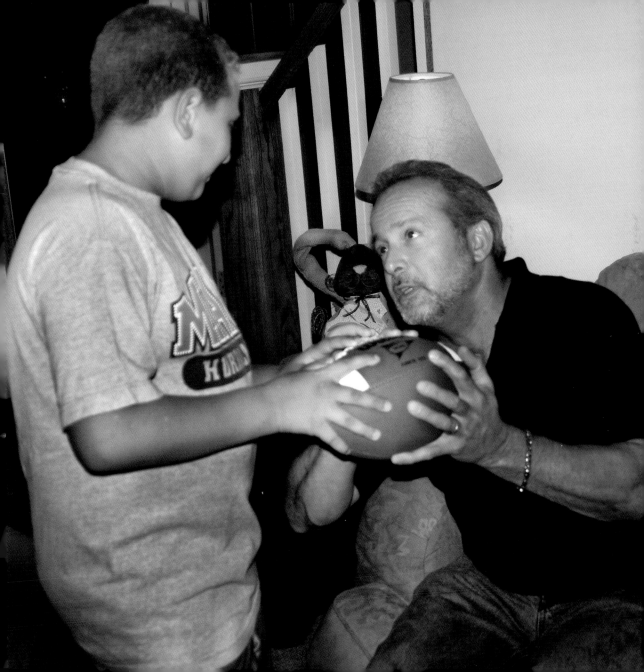

Grandchildren

help grandfathers tap into their creative side.

Grandfathers

proudly display grandchildren's artwork.

Grandfathers help grandchildren

build a fort in the backyard.

Grandchildren tell grandfathers

what goes where.

Grandfathers

give grandchildren countless hugs and kisses.

Grandchildren

love being cuddled by grandfathers.

Grandsons

help grandfathers blow out the candles.

Grandfathers

teach grandsons to celebrate every day.

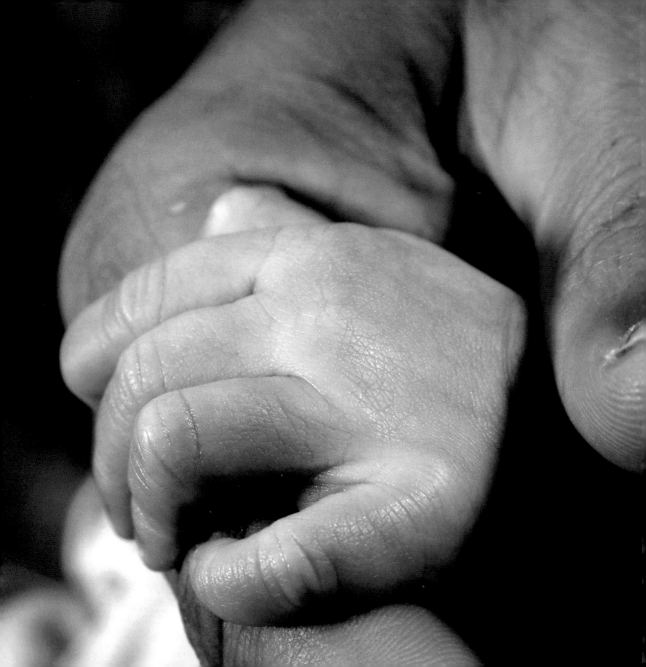

Grandchildren teach grandfathers

when to hold on and when to let go.

Grandfathers remind grandchildren

that they're always there to lend a hand.

Grandchildren tell grandfathers

their dreams and wishes.

Grandfathers assure grandchildren

that the sky's the limit.

Grandfathers love grandchildren

unconditionally.

Grandchildren monopolize grandfathers

when they come to visit.

Grandfathers tell grandchildren

funny stories about their parents.

Grandchildren beg grandfathers

to tell them more.

Grandchildren

tell grandfathers the latest jokes.

Grandfathers

always laugh at the right places.

Grandfathers

love spoiling grandchildren.

Grandchildren

know that when grandfathers are around,

it's time to play.

Grandchildren remind grandfathers

of their own youth.

Grandfathers encourage grandchildren

to take interest in family history.

Grandchildren

ask grandfathers to play catch.

Grandfathers

tickle grandchildren after a tackle.

Grandfathers

share their wisdom with grandchildren.

Grandchildren

bond with grandfathers over common interests.

Grandchildren remind grandfathers

to be silly sometimes.

Grandfathers show grandchildren

just how silly they can be.

Grandfathers give grandchildren

a boost after a tough day.

Grandchildren make grandfathers

smile from ear-to-ear.